Let your imagination expand beyond the pages of this book.

COLOURS & SHAPES

ACTIVITY BOOK

Marcus Walters

Play, make and explore art at www.tate.org.uk/kids

TATE

Hide and Seek

Can you spot these shapes
throughout the book?

Can you add the names of these shapes
and then find the matching stickers?

....

....

What is your
favourite shape?
Draw it here.

Square

Heart

Semicircle

Triangle

Star

Circle

Wiggly Worms

Complete the patterns using your stickers.

Shape City

This picture is made of lots of different shapes.
Colour it in and then count the shapes.

Mix It Up

When you mix colours together you can make brand new colours. What colours will you get if you mix:

Add your own . . .

Smart Shapes

Can you draw the shapes in the boxes
below and then colour them in?

Red Circle

Purple Square

Green Rectangle

Blue Diamond

Orange Triangle

Yellow Heart

Colour by Shape

Can you colour all the:
Triangles – Blue
Squares – Red
Stars – Yellow
Circles – Green

Colour by Numbers

1
1
1
1
1
1
2
1
1
3
3
1
4
3
3
5

1 2 3 4 5

Colour Codes

Each player should pick a different coloured pencil and place their counter on the start. Take it in turns to roll the dice and move forward the number shown. Then follow the instruction for that number. For example, if you a roll a 2 – you move forward two spaces and colour a triangle. The winner is the person who has coloured in the most shapes at the finish.

Start

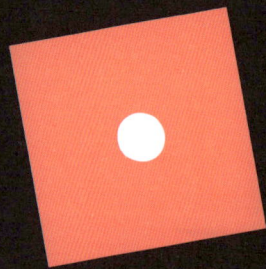

Miss a turn

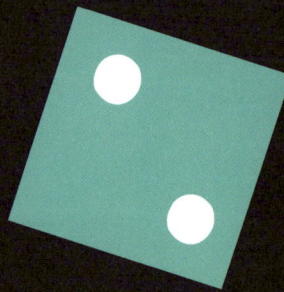

Triangle

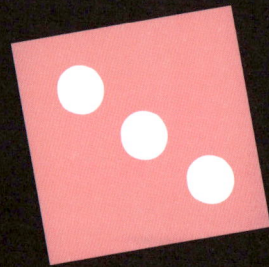

Circle

Square

You choose!

Colour in someone else's shape!

Finish

Bright Butterfly

Colour the shapes: red blue green

Wonderful Words

Can you trace and write the names of the shapes?

 circle ....

 triangle ....

 square ....

 rectangle ....

 oval ....

Your masterpiece!

Match the correct stickers to the numbers to complete the picture.

Sticker key:

 3
 4
 5
 6

17

Can you see me in 3D?

Colour the shapes using the key below.

Cone = Yellow

Cylinder = Blue

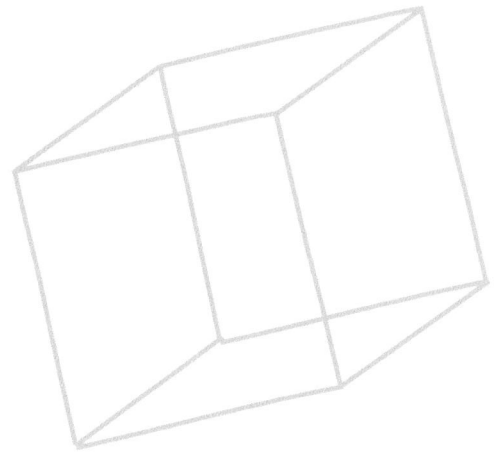

Cube = Red

Draw some everyday objects that use these shapes . . .

Ice cream

Birthday present

Bottle

What am I?

Find the right shape and add a sticker.

I have 0 corners,
I am easy to roll.

I have 4 corners,
I have 4 sides.

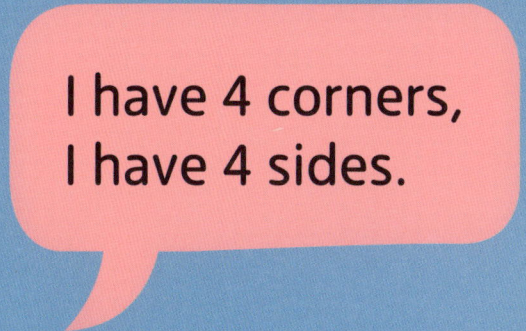

I have 3 corners,
I have 3 sides.

Animal magic

Add some shapes to
these animals to make
them more colourful.

You can create your favourite animals using only shapes!
Why don't you try it below with your stickers?

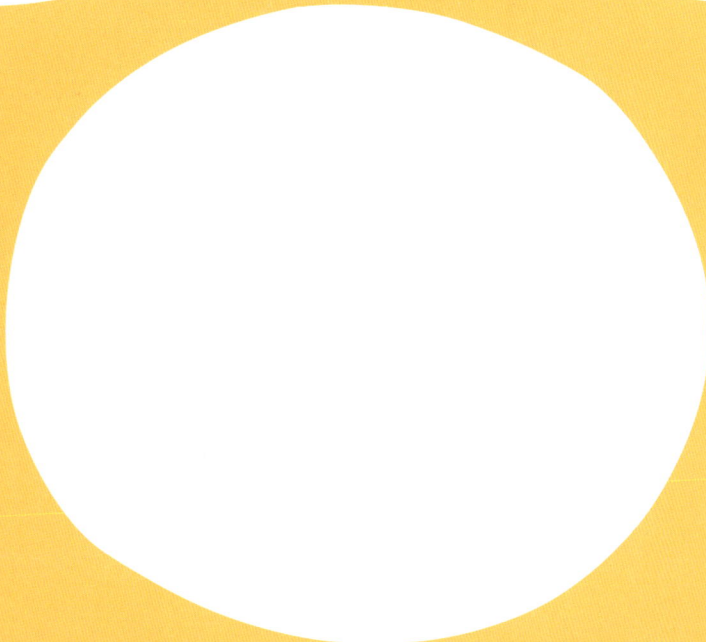

Your self portrait

Create your own pictures using any leftover stickers.

Time for ice cream

Decorate your ice cream with sprinkles and shapes.

First published 2018 by order of the Tate Trustees
by Tate Publishing, a division of Tate Enterprises Ltd,
Millbank, London SW1P 4RG
www.tate.org.uk/publishing
Illustrations © Marcus Walters 2018
Text © Tate Enterprises 2018

First published 2018
A catalogue record for this book is available from the British Library
ISBN 978 1 84976 571 8

Distributed in the United States and Canada by ABRAMS, New York
Library of Congress Control Number applied for
Printed and bound in China by C&C Offset Printing Co., Ltd
Colour reproduction by DL Imaging Ltd, London

Stickers!

More stickers